LIFE CYCLE OF A FROG

By Kirsty Holmes

LIFE CYCLES

Words that look like **this** can be found in the glossary on page 24.

©2018
Book Life
King's Lynn
Norfolk PE30 4LS

Written by:
Kirsty Holmes

Edited by:
Holly Duhig

Designed by:
Daniel Scase

ISBN: 978-1-78637-284-0

All rights reserved
Printed in Malaysia

A catalogue record for this book is available from the British Library.

PHOTO CREDITS

Photocredits: Abbreviations: l-left, r-right, b-bottom, t-top, c-centre, m-middle. Front Cover – Hintau Aliaksei, bg – perlphoto. 1m – Hintau Aliaksei, bg – perlphoto. 3 – Linus T. 3bg – perlphoto, 3tr – DJTaylor, 3mr – bluecrayola, 3br – davemhuntphotography. 4l – Oksana Kuzmina, 4m – Dmitry Lobanov, 4r – Pressmaster. 5l – Alliance, 5m – Elnur, 5r – Josep Curto. 6 – Rudmer Zwerver. 7 – Aleksey Stemmer. 8 – Roy Pederson. 9 – Ian Grainger. 10 – vvoe. 11 – Dr Morley Read. 12 – Jay Ondreicka. 13 – kungfoofoto. 14 – Freebilly. 15 – davemhuntphotography. 16 – Krisda Ponchaipulltawee. 17 – Cathy Keifer. 18tl – reptiles4all, 18br – Dirk Ercken. 19tr – Ficmajstr, 19br – Rudmer Zwerver. 20 – Mircea C. 21 – Choke29. 22l – Peter Baxter. 22m – Edvard Mizsei 22-23m – Steve Byland. 23m – Daniele Carotenuto. 23r – Gerald A. DeBoer.
Images are courtesy of Shutterstock.com. With thanks to Getty Images, Thinkstock Photo and iStockphoto

All facts, statistics, web addresses and URLs in this book were verified as valid and accurate at time of writing. No responsibility for any changes to external websites or references can be accepted by either the author or publisher.

LIFE CYCLE OF A FROG

Page 4	What Is a Life Cycle?
Page 6	Fantastic Frogs
Page 8	Excellent Eggs
Page 10	Terrific Tadpoles
Page 12	Fun Froglets
Page 14	Funky Frogs
Page 16	Life as a Frog
Page 18	Fun Facts about Frogs
Page 20	The End of Life as a Frog
Page 22	The Life Cycle
Page 24	Glossary and Index

WHAT IS A LIFE CYCLE?

All living things have a life cycle. They are all born, they all grow bigger, and their bodies change.

Baby

Toddler

Child

When they are fully grown, they have **offspring** of their own. In the end, all living things die. This is the life cycle.

Teenager

Adult

Elderly Person

FANTASTIC FROGS

Frogs are amphibians. This means they live both on land and in water. Frogs are **cold-blooded**, with short front legs and long, powerful back legs. Most have sticky tongues for catching flies to eat.

Frogs have webbed feet, which help them to swim.

Sticky Tongue

Front Legs

Webbed Feet

Back Legs

Frogs have many **predators** who like to eat them. Because of this, they have lots of ways of protecting themselves. Some frogs are brightly-coloured, which tells predators they are poisonous to eat.

Golden Poison Arrow Frog

Other frogs can use their colours to blend in and hide.

EXCELLENT EGGS

Female frogs lay eggs, called frogspawn. The female will look for a safe spot to lay her eggs. Each egg contains a frog **embryo**, and jelly for it to eat.

Most frogs lay their eggs in water. Some **species** lay them under leaves, and others keep them on their bodies.

Embryo

Frogspawn needs light and warmth to grow.

Frog eggs are kept together in a big clump of jelly. A female frog might lay thousands of eggs at a time! Only a few eggs will make it – the rest will be eaten by predators.

TERRIFIC TADPOLES

About three weeks after the eggs are laid, the embryos will have formed a head, **gills**, and tail. They then hatch out of the eggs as tadpoles.

Head

Tail

Gills

Tadpoles eat the jelly in the eggs for **nutrients.**

Tadpoles grow and change a lot. When they hatch, they look almost like fish. But as they eat, they develop legs and other **characteristics**, and lose their tails. This change is called 'metamorphosis'.

FUN FROGLETS

Tadpoles turn into small frogs, called 'froglets'. This change can happen very suddenly – sometimes overnight!

Froglets eat living things and will soon need to start catching flies.

Froglets form lungs and can live outside of the water. At this stage they start to explore the land.

Froglets look like tiny frogs, and not like fish anymore!

FUNKY FROGS

Between 12 and 16 weeks old, the frog becomes an adult. Adult frogs are very good at swimming, jumping and catching food to eat.

Some frogs live on the ground. Others, like this red-eyed Amazon tree frog, live in trees. They have bulging eyes so they can see all around them.

LIFE AS A FROG

Adult frogs will look for a **mate**, and have offspring of their own. Adult females will lay their own eggs, often in the same place they were born.

Tomato Frogs

Frogs like to eat bugs, spiders, worms, slugs and even small fish! They catch them with their long, sticky tongues, which flick out very fast to catch their **prey**.

FUN FACTS ABOUT FROGS

- One golden poison dart frog has enough poison in its skin to kill ten grown men.

- The world's largest frog is the Goliath frog. It can weigh up to 3.5 kilograms. That's as much as a newborn baby!

- The glass frog has skin which is so see-through you can see its heart beating!

- **The smallest frog is the P.amauensis which is only seven millimetres long!**

- A group of frogs is called an 'army'.

- **Some male frogs croak to attract females. They have a sac under their mouth which fills with air. Some frog croaks can be heard a long way away!**

THE END OF LIFE AS A FROG

Some species of frog can live for a long time. Most species of frog live between 4 to 15 years, but some have lived for much longer.

Some bullfrogs have been known to live to 40 years old.

Frogs have lots of predators to watch out for. Birds, owls, weasels, otters, foxes, snakes and large fish all like to eat frogs. Cats and dogs can also prey on frogs.

THE LIFE CYCLE

Frogspawn

Tadpole

A frog's life cycle has different stages.
All the stages are different.

Froglet

Frog

Bigger Tadpole

The frogspawn hatches into a tadpole. The tadpole changes into an adult frog through metamorphosis. The adult frog has offspring of its own.

In the end, the frog dies, and the life cycle is complete.

GLOSSARY

camouflage	traits that allow an animal to hide itself in a habitat
characteristics	features of a thing that help to identify it
cold-blooded	animals that have blood which changes with the temperature around them
embryo	an unborn or unhatched young in the process of development
gills	the organs that some animals use to breathe underwater
mate	a partner (of the same species) who an animal chooses to produce young with
nutrients	natural substances that animals and humans need to grow and stay healthy
offspring	the child, or young, of a living thing
predators	animals that hunt other animals for food
prey	animals that are hunted by other animals for food
species	a group of very similar animals or plants that are capable of producing young together

INDEX

camouflage 21
croaking 19
embryo 8-10
flies 6, 12
frogspawn 8-9, 22-23

jumping 14
legs 6, 11
lungs 13
metamorphosis 11, 23
poison 7, 18

swimming 14
tongues 6, 17
water 6, 8, 13